SENIOR CITIZENS'
GOOD FOOD GUIDE
TO DERBYSHIRE

WHERE TO FIND QUALITY FOOD
AT VALUE-FOR-MONEY PRICES
2006-2007

JEN EDGAR & DICK RICHARDSON

ASHRIDGE PRESS

Published for:
The Senior Citizens' Good Food Guides
182 Brown Edge Road, Buxton, Derbyshire SK17 7AA
e-mail: jennifer.edgar@tesco.net
by:
Ashridge Press, Courtyard Cottage, Little Longstone, Bakewell, Derbyshire DE45 1NN
Tel/Fax: 01629 640670   e-mail: dickrichardson@country-books.co.uk

ISBN 1 901214 51 6
© 2006 Jen Edgar and Dick Richardson

All details were correct when this book went to press,
but the Senior Citizens' Good Food Guide and Ashridge Press
cannot accept liability for any changes in facilities
or prices subsequently made.
If you are making a special journey to an establishment in these
pages, we advise that you telephone the venue first.

*Not all place-names appear on the map
and it should be used only as a guide to location.*

Printed and bound:
Gutenberg Press Ltd

CONTENTS

Introduction

Welcome to the 2006-2007 SENIOR CITIZENS' GOOD FOOD GUIDE for Derbyshire!

Why another Food Guide? What's different about this one? A great deal, in every sense.

Now you're a Senior Citizen you have a bit more time to explore the beautiful county of Derbyshire. There is something for everyone, whether you enjoy wandering round villages, walking the hills, exploring architectural gems or taking in some retail therapy in a garden centre or one of our larger towns. Having a meal out adds to the pleasure of a day out. But – it can be expensive.

The Senior Citizens' Good Food Guide will show you where to find the best food at difficult-to-beat prices. From standard roast dinners to bacon and egg baps, delicious Italian food to smaller portions of your favourites, they are all here in the Guide.

There are olde-worlde pubs with beamed ceilings and open fires to Italian restaurants with an ambience that makes you feel you are in Italy. There are garden centres where you can combine your love of plants and flowers with a delicious lunch. Whatever your ideal eating place you'll find something to please you in the Food Guide.

Add to that interesting facts about the towns and villages; did you know that there is a wild flower nursery at Grindleford or that Florence Nightingale was a frequent visitor to Whatstand-well? Or that DH Lawrence drew on the atmosphere and people of the Middleton area for his novels and Joan Eyre built a tower in Stoney Middleton to commemorate and celebrate her husband's safe return from Agincourt in 1415?

The Food Guide gives you all this and more.

So whether it's the spring and summer sunshine or the crisp autumn and winter days that make you want to get out and about, we hope you'll find those special eating places that won't break the bank but will add to the enjoyment of your day.

Jen Edgar and Dick Richardson
2006

We plan to update this book on a regular basis, so if we have omitted your favourite place, then please let us know. We would also like to know if any details in this book have changed since going to press. We welcome your recommendations for establishments that offer special deals for Senior Citizens anywhere in the country – not just Derbyshire, as this is the first of a series of guides covering the country. You will find our address at the end of the book.

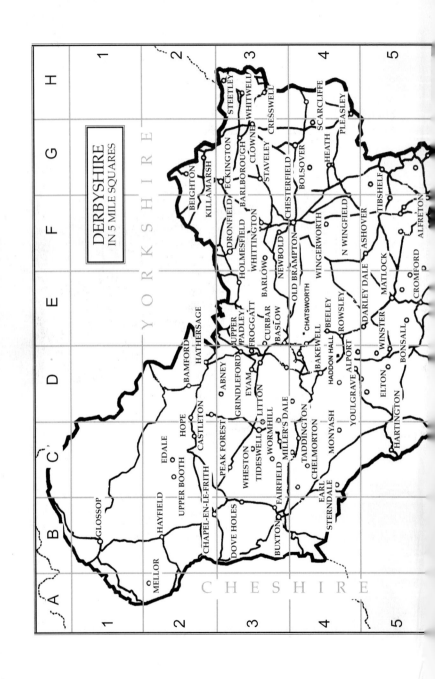

DERBYSHIRE
IN 5 MILE SQUARES

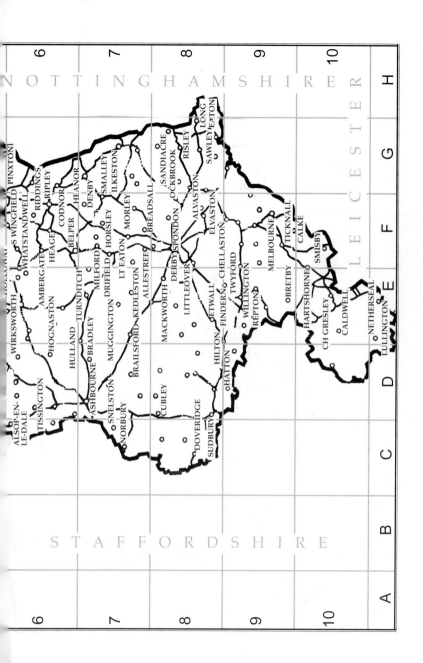

ALFRETON

A market town with no pretensions to uniformity or beauty in its buildings is seated on a small ridge. The manufacture of stockings was once an important local industry and the former ironworks of James Oakes was famous for some of the largest iron bridges and the casting of cannons. Map F6.

Rachell's Restaurant, Hilcote Lane, Hilcote, Alfreton Tel: 01773 811248. Thursday meal offer. Tea and coffee. Wheelchair access.

Tudor Rose Restaurant, Central Road, Alfreton Tel: 01773 832795. Meal offer Monday – Friday.

The Old Grammar School, Church Street

The gateway to Dovedale, this attractive little market town boasts among its past visitors Charles I, Bonny Prince Charlie, James Boswell, Samuel Johnson, Thomas Moore, George Eliot, Isaac Walton and Jean Jacques Rosseau. Church Street, with its buildings of every period from the 16th to the 18th centuries, is recognised by many as one of the most perfect townscapes in the country and St Oswald's church has a graceful 212ft stone spire. The First World War poet Francis St Vincent Morris who died in the trenches aged 21, was the son of a former vicar. The old 16th century grammar school has been converted into apartments and two groups of beautiful old almshouses remain. A stalls market is held every Thursday. Shrovetide Football still takes place every year and the ball was recently 'thrown up' by the Prince of Wales. Map D7.

Smith's Tavern, 36 St John's Street, Ashbourne Tel: 01335 342264. A 16th century olde worlde pub with oak beamed interior, separate dining room and no loud music! Meal offer £4.95 plus free tea and coffee Monday – Friday 12 noon – 2.45pm. Steak and kidney pie, roast beef, cod and plaice. Disabled access and toilets. Coaches and mini-buses by arrangement.

BAKEWELL

A pretty town on the river Wye, famous for its puddings. Market day is Monday with stalls selling fruit, vegetables and general goods in the town and the sheep and cattle market just over the river at the new agricultural centre. Bakewell Show is held in August and the original one-day fair has been stretched to two. A good base for visiting two nearby stately homes – Chatsworth House and Haddon Hall. There is a charming small museum in a Tudor tax collectors house and the church boasts monuments to the Vernon and Manners families, ancestors of the Dukes of Rutland. The Old Market Hall, now an information centre, was erected by the Manners family and their shield adorns the outside of the building. Lady Manners founded a grammar school in 1636. Just out of town at Rowsley is

Caldwell's Mill, which has been a working mill for over 400 years. Map D4.

Australian Bar Diner, Granby Road, Bakewell Offers meals for pensioners at £4.95 – and not a kangaroo steak in sight! Tea and coffee. Licensed. Public disabled toilet opposite the premises.

Farmer's Feast Café and Bar, Agricultural Centre, Coombs Road, Bakewell offers Sunday lunch at £5.50.

BAMFORD

The sole survivor of three villages – Ashopton and Derwent, in the valley, were flooded to form the Ladybower reservoir, where Sir Barnes Wallis tested the 'bouncing' bomb. A former mill village, the wells are dressed in mid-July. The former mill on the river Derwent, built in 1791, has been converted into apartments. Near the station can be found the Mytham Bridge toll gate, moved here by the Peak Park. Built in 1758 for the first turnpike in the area, linking Sheffield with Sparrowpit. Thornhill House was once a seat of the Eyre family. Map D2.

The Anglers Rest, Main Road, Bamford Tel: 01433 651424 Lynda and Ian provide 2 course lunches for £3.25 with a choice of rump steak, chicken breast or fresh fish. Disabled access. Garden. Tea and coffee. Coaches welcome.

Barlborough Hall

The village lies on the borders of Yorkshire, 3 miles from
Eckington and 8 miles NE from Chesterfield, off the A619.
Formerly the main industries were coal and iron-stone mining.
Barlborough Hall was built in 1583 by Lord Justice Francis
Rodes, one of the judges at the trial of Mary Queen of Scots. It
was designed by Robert Smythson, architect of Hardwick Hall.
The 13th century church was heavily restored in 1899 and the
village has some charmng old stone houses with pantile roofs.
The custom of well dressing was revived in the village in 1975
and is normally held around St James' Day (25th July), to whom
the church is dedicated. Map G4.

The Royal Oak, High Street, Barlborough S43 4EU Tel: 01246 573020. This inn dates from the early 1800's Meal offers Monday – Friday 12 noon – 5pm. The early evening menu Moday – Friday 5 – 7pm offers two main meals for £10. Diasabled access.

BARTON-UNDER-NEEDWOOD

Just over the border in Staffordshire on rising ground above the river Trent. It is 15 miles south of Derby.

The New Inn, Five Ends Lane, Burton Road, Needwood Tel: 01283 575392. This inn, built in 1760, lies 4 miles W from Burton and 3 miles N of Barton-under-Needwood. Smaller protions are offered for pensioners and include cod and chips at £3.85 and shepherds pie for £3.65. Tea and coffee.

Baslow

Baslow is a pretty village set in delightful countryside yet within easy reach of Sheffield, Chesterfield and the Peak District. An ideal stopping place for visitors to Chatsworth House, it lies on the A619 between Chesterfield and Bakewell. Dr. Wrench was responsible for erecting the 10ft high gritstone cross known as Wellington's Monument at 1,000ft on Baslow Edge in 1866. High on the opposite Birchen Edge stands Nelson's Pole, erected in 1810 by John Brightman, another Baslow man. Baslow Hall stands in landscaped grounds just off the A623 north of the village. Built in 1907 for Rev. Jeremiah Stockdale who was vicar of Baslow for 48 years, it became the home of electrical pioneer Sebastian de Ferranti in 1913 until his death in 1930. Map E3.

The Devonshire Arms, Nether End, Baslow Tel: 01246 582551. A family-run hotel on the A619 offering deals on meals. Tea and coffee. Disabled access and toilets. Coaches and mini-buses by arrangement.

The Robin Hood Inn, Chesterfield Road, Baslow Tel: 01246 583186. Dates from the 17th century. Meal offers Monday – Friday lunchtimes. Tea and coffee.

The Wheatsheaf Hotel, Nether End, Baslow, DE45 1SR Tel: 01246 582240. On the A619, The Wheatsheaf Hotel offers Senior Citizens deals all day and everyday. We can particularly recommend their delicious home made pies and their wide ranging menu includes vegetarian dishes. Full table service, tea and coffee as well as alcoholic drinks make it a popular choice for anyone enjoying the lovely scenery in this part of Derbyshire. Coach and mini-bus parties are welcome but need to pre-book. There is good access to toilet facilities.

Until 1776, this small town was known for making nails. When Jedediah Strutt came, he built his six cotton mills here in order to harness the water power of the River Derwent. The fine stone bridge dates from 1795 and replaces others washed away by floods. The North Mill is now a World Heritage site and is open to the public. When George Stephenson brought the railway here, Mr Strutt did not wish to see the trains – they were hidden from view in cuttings. The river makes a crescent waterfall on its way to the gorge beyond the bridge. Map F7.

The Hollybush Inn, Holly Bush Lane, Makeney, Belper DE56 0RX Tel: 01332 841729. An old Grade II listed inn where the beer is still brought from the cellar in jugs – pure nostalgia for those of us who remember when many pubs were like this! Lunches Monday – Friday, pie and chips or fish and chips – smaller portions at lower prices. Tea and coffee. Disabled access.

BIRCH VALE

A village in the High Peak near New Mills and Hayfield, it includes the attached village of Thornsett, and is just outside the boundary of the Peak District National Park. The railway station closed in 1970 and the trackbed now carries the Sett Valley Trail. TV presenter Tess Daly was born here. Map B3.

The Waltzing Weasel Inn, Birch Vale, High Peak Recently taken over by the former landlord of The Homesford Cottage Inn, Whatstandwell. His high standards have come with him and there are meal offers Monday – Saturday lunchtimes. Two courses for £6.50 – starter and main course or main course and dessert. Good quality produce is always used – no frozen vegetables or 'cheap meat' here. There is a large choice of vegetarian food and tea and coffee are served. The pub is set in pleasant gardens with dramatic views and was voted 'Derbyshire dining pub of the year' 1997-98, 2000, 2002-04. Coaches and mini-buses by arrangement.

The Vine Tavern, Highfield Road, Birch Vale, High Peak Tel: 01663 741021. A range of home-cooked food for pensioners. Tea and coffee.

Bolsover Castle

Once a market town, it lies 6 miles east of Chesterfield. The mines and other industry have disappeared and the valley below is once again lush green. It is overlooked by the castle (English Heritage) built by Sir Charles Cavendish, son of Bess of Hardwick, in 1613-16. The site was once a Norman castle and commands an impressive position. Charles I was entertained here on three occasions. Apart from the keep tower and the indoor riding school, the other buildings are roofless ruins. Peter Fidler was born here and worked for the Hudson Bay Company, mapping a great part of Canada. (See *True Brit* by Gordon Jackson published by Country Books.) Map G5.

Castle Fish Bar, Market Place, Bolsover 10% discount on food.

BRADWELL

At the heart of the Peak District, the unspoilt village of Bradwell, known locally as Bradda, is a village on a hillside. The Roman road of Batham Gate which ran between Aqua Arnemetia (Buxton) and Anavio (Brough) passes less than a mile to the north. The earliest of Bradwell's substantial dwellings is from the Tudor period; with a date stone of 1549 atop the coat of arms of the Vernon and Swynnerton families carved above the five-arched mullioned windows on its west gable, Hazelbadge Hall stands at the roadside, now part of a large farm complex on the outskirts of the village at the southern end of Bradwell Dale. Two hundred years ago there were several hat manufacturers here and Bradwell was famous for both its fashionable felt hats and the 'Bradda Beaver' – a hard hat favoured by miners. The most benevolent benefactor and also it's most famous son was George Fox, inventor of the folding umbrella frame. Tiny cottages and narrow lanes make it a pleasure to explore and a trip to Bagshawe Cavern is well worthwhile. (see *Bradwell, Ancient & Modern* by Seth Evans, published in 1912 and reprinted by Country Books 2004.) As a treat, try the famous – and wonderful – Bradwell Dairy Ice Cream. Map C3.

Ye Olde Bowling Green Inn, Smalldale, Bradwell, Hope Valley, S33 9JQ Tel: 01433 620450. A former coaching inn with parts dating from the 16th century. Tea and coffee.

BREADSALL

The village lies on a hillside above the River Derwent. The stately Breadsall Priory dating from the 17th century is now a hotel with a fine golf course. Here the Darwin family lived from 1799-1858 – Erasmus Darwin, physician, poet and philosopher, died here in 1802. He was the grandfather of Charles Darwin. Map F8.

The Paddock, 391 Mansfield Road, Breadsall DE21 4AW Tel: 01332 833592. Offers a Golden Years menu Monday – Friday lunchtimes. Tea and coffee.

BULLBRIDGE

Lying between the river Amber and the Cromford canal, this hillside village ia a mile from Crich with its world-famous tram museum. It is dominated by Stevenson's Dye Works, founded on Wirksworth Moor in 1825 by James Stevenson. The last two family members resigned from the board in the 1960's and is now part of the Coats group. The village, with a population of 220 people, has lost many of its old buildings including a watermill used for grinding flour. Map F7.

The Canal Inn, Bullbridge Hill, Bullbridge, Belper Tel: 01773 852739. Dating from the 18th century, the inn lies close to the Cromford Canal. Meal offer weekdays with vegetarian alternatives. Tea and coffee.

The Crescent, Buxton

For many the Jewel in the Crown of the High Peak area of Derbyshire. A spa town full of historic buildings, with an 23 acre park and the Pavilion Gardens and Opera House, it is a magnet for the tourist. Add to the overall atmosphere of a market town the Buxton Festival and Fringe and you'll understand why it is a perfect place as a base to explore the Peak District or for a day visit. Map B3.

The Pavilion Gardens Tel: 01298 77777 is a stunning park with a Victorian-style bandstand and a fountain set amidst ancient trees and the river Wye running through it. The Pavilion Gardens Restaurant offers very good food in a pleasant, airy, ground floor wheelchair-friendly restaurant. Pensioners offers are available on Tuesdays – Thursdays for £5. Tea and coffee.

If your preference is for a touch of the Italian without the hassle of actually going there then **Michelangelo's, 1, Market Place, Buxton SK17 6EB** Tel: 01298 26640 is the perfect place. The newly furbished restaurant has a reputation for very high

The Pavilion, Buxton

quality food, served in a delightful restaurant with friendly and helpful staff. Sunday through to Thursday evenings, 6-7pm all pizzas and pasta dishes are £3.99. There is a wide choice of food, including vegetarian, and most dietary needs can be accommodated. To help you choose your food new, larger print menus are offered. There is a downstairs bathroom for people with disabilities. Private dining is available for up to 40 people. Coach and mini bus parties are catered for and there is ample public parking opposite the restaurant.

Hydro Tea-Rooms, Spring Gardens, Buxton In the centre of the shopping area the Hydro offers basic food at affordable prices. Bacon and egg cobs, Welsh rarebit and toasted tea cakes give a flavour of the menu. There is the normal selection of non-alcoholic drinks. There is a 15% discount for Gold Card holders.

The King's Head, Market Place, Buxton SK17 6EJ Tel: 01298 27719. Monday – Saturday from 12 noon – 3pm. Tea and coffee. Disabled access up small step.

The Old Hall Hotel, Water Street, Buxton Famous for being a resting place for Mary, Queen of Scots, this hotel has everything you need for a day out. There is a good variety of food offered with some delicious sweets. Pensioner deals include two-for-the-price-of-one main courses Monday – Friday and a 10% discount at weekends.

The Railway Hotel, Bridge Street, Buxton. Town centre location within a few minutes walk of the shops and Pavilion Gardens offering good food. Tea and coffee.

The Robin Hood, London Road, Buxton. Good food and very nice atmosphere.

The Opera House, Buxton

BUXWORTH

A small village situated between New Mills, Hayfield and Chapel-en-le-Frith known as Buggesworth from 1222 after the Bugge family from Nottinghamshire. Ralph de Bugge was bailiff of the king's Peak Forest which extended to 180 square miles. Bugsworth Hall was built in 1627. The Peak Forest canal arrived here in 1798 and declined in the 1920's. Limestone was transported by a tramway from Dove Holes quarry to Bugsworth Canal Basin. The village changed the name Bugsworth to Buxworth in 1929. Map B3.

The Navigation Inn, Bugsworth Basin, Buxworth, near Whaley Bridge, High Peak Tel: 01663 732072. A 200 year-old pub on a canal basin with lots of interesting memorabilia. Good snacks and traditional home-made meals at reasonable prices. Vegetarian dishes and tea and coffee are available. Log fires in the winter assure a warm welcome. Groups should pre-book. Facilities for disabled. You can also order food to be ready after your walk. In the 1970s the pub belonged to Pat Phoenix – Elsie Tanner of TVs *Coronation Street*.

CALVER

It lies mainly on the west bank of the Derwent in a triangle between the A623 and the B6001, 5 miles north of Bakewell. A cotton mill was built near Calver Bridge in 1778 by Thomas Pares of Risley and John Gardom of Bubnell, and in 1785 Gardom built another, much larger mill close by. But tragedy struck twice within the space of three years when the 300 year-old bridge was swept away during the disastrous floods of 1799, and then the larger of Gardom's two cotton mills burned down completely in 1802. Lead mining and lime burning were the early industries, and a boot factory making steel-capped footwear for miners, closed at the end of the 20th century. Calver Mill built in 1805 is now converted to apartments – familiar to many people from its use by BBC TV as the castle in Colditz. There is an excellent craft centre at Calver Bridge. Map D4.

The Eyre Arms, Calver Sough S32 3XH Tel: 01433 630473. Set on the edge of the small village of Calver, 4 miles from Bakewell. Steve and Rita serve a wide variety of excellent food. Pensioners lunches are £6.95 for two courses 12 noon – 3pm. The same menu is available in the evenings from 6pm – 7pm at

£7.95 – perfect for a special celebration. Tea and coffee. Disabled access. The indoor and outdoor facilities for the grandchildren include an animal farm. Well worth a visit is the Calver Sough Garden Centre opposite the pub.

The village is a magnet for people who enjoy the stunning show caves, where a pillar of Blue John stone can be viewed, the variety of gift shops and the surrounding countryside. The village is a tourist attraction throughout the year and is particularly beautiful in the Christmas season when the shops, lit by fairy lights, make you feel you are back in Charles Dicken's days. William Peverill, a friend of William the Conqueror, built the castle here which is now in the custody of English Heritage. Sir Walter Scott made the castle famous by his novel *Peverill of the Peak*. Peak Cavern is open from April – October. Don't miss Garland Day on 29th May. Formerly Jack-in-the-Green or the Green Man and held on May 1st, the date was changed to commemorate Charles II hiding in an oak tree after the Battle of Worcester. Map C2.

The Bulls Head Hotel, Cross Street, Castleton, Hope Valley

S33 8WH Tel: 01433 620256 Transformed and refurbished by Karen and Lynn it still retains its original character. Chef, Dale Edwards has worked at the Grove Hotel, Buxton and is well-known in the area. Lunches Monday-Friday. Tea and coffee. Wheelchair access from car park at rear of premises. Disabled toilets.

After a day spent exploring all that Castleton has to offer it would be shame just to drive off home, especially when the Peaks Inn is graded with four diamonds. This homely village pub with leather armchairs assures you of a good welcome. **The Peaks Inn, How Lane, Castleton, Hope Valley S3S 8WJ** Tel: 01433 620247, e-mail: info@peaks-inn.co.uk. The Peaks Inn prides itself on providing hearty meals at affordable prices. You can be sure of a warm welcome from friendly staff. They offer a light bites menu, a vegetarian dish or a larger meal. Tea and coffee are also served. There is ample parking for coach and mini bus parties and, an added bonus, the driver eats free. An

additional plus for The Peaks Inn is that they welcome dogs. There is a beer garden at the rear of the inn where you can enjoy summer days and warm, balmy evenings. Disabled access and toilets.

A little stone town on the slopes of a fertile valley with an old-world market place, ancient cross and stocks. Now by-passed from the Buxton to Stockport road, it is well worth the detour. The name comes from the foresters and keepers of the old Forest of the Peak who built a chapel here nearly 800 years ago. Chapel Brow, a steep cobbled lane, leads from the church to Market Street. A curious custom has survived, and freeholders of land in the parish are allowed to choose their own vicar. In 1648 the church was used to hold 1,500 Scottish prisoners for 16 days. The conditions led to the death of 44 men. Map B3.

The Beehive, Combs, near Chapel-en-le-Frith The tiny village of Combs boasts one of the most popular pubs in the area. Old world surroundings don't mean dull food. A wide variety of dishes, including vegetarian are on offer at lunch times. Soup and a roll followed by a main course is offered for £5.50 for pensioners Monday – Thursday. Its popularity makes it advisable to book before making your journey.

The Cinnamon Restaurant & Takeaway, Market Street, Chapel-en-le-Frith Tel: 01298 814597. 10% discount.

Ye Olde Stocks Café, Chapel-en-le-Frith. Run by a very friendly young couple who provide home-made meals at reasonable prices. They are willing to cater for special diets.

Chatsworth House and Garden Map E4. The new Duke of Devonshire, the twelfth, has rearranged the state rooms to reflect the period of the first duke. There is also a new exhibition celebrating the life and collecting of his father, the eleventh duke. Open Easter to December 21st, 11am – 5.30pm. Tel: 01246 582204.

The Vines Restaurant, Chatsworth Garden Centre, Calton Lees, Chatsworth Tel: 01629 734004. No special deals for senior citizens but the garden centre is a must for the plant or gift hunter – especially at Christmas. Tea and coffee. Wheelchair access and disabled toilet.

CHELLASTON

Now a suburb south of the city of Derby. In this village, from the 14th century onwards, the slabs of white alabaster were quarried for carving into tombs that feature in many of England's cathedrals and churches. Gypsum deposits were found and a thriving brick and plaster industry developed. JS Gresley and his son, Frank, were noted 19th century landscape painters and Cuthbert, Frank's son, was a well known porcelain painter at Royal Crown Derby. In March 1947, a local man was killed by a hurricane. Map F9.

The Bonnie Prince, 166 Swarkestone Road, Chellaston, Derby DE73 5UE Tel: 01335 702275. A Hardys and Hansons house converted in 2000 and extended in 2004 to seat around 250 people. Lunches Monday – Saturday 11am – 5pm. Haddock in parsley sauce, liver and onions, sausage and mash – smaller portions at lower prices are available for pensioners. Vegetarian alternatives from main menu. Tea and coffee. Wheelchair access. Disabled toilets. Beer garden. Coaches and mini-busses by arrangement.

Known all over the world for its church with the crooked spire – the framework was built from unseasoned wood and covered in lead plates. Opposite the church is the Chesterfield Museum and Art Gallery which houses paintings by Joseph Syddall, who lived at Whittington. It was here that the Victorian engineer, George Stephenson, came to live after the construction of the Midland Railway line. Market Place is dominated by the Victorian Hall erected in 1857. The Peacock Heritage Centre is housed in the former Peacock Inn and dates from 1500. The stalls market survives four days a week, and on Thursdays a flea market is held. Chesterfield Canal, built by James Brindley in 1771, is currently under-going restoration. Map F4.

Applewood Inn, Springbank Road, Chesterfield Tel: 01246 550542. Meal offers Thursday lunchtime only. Wheelchair access.

Blue Star Cafe, Mansfield Road, Hasland, Chesterfield Meal offers Monday – Friday.

Boot & Shoe, North Wingfield Road, Grassmoor, Chesterfield Tel: 01246 850251. 25% discount on food lunchtimes.

The Golden Fleece, 9 High Street, Chesterfield S40 1PS Tel: 01246 208596 Pensioners Monday – Saturday 11am – 3pm.

Wheelchair access to front. Coaches by appointment.

The Highfield, Newbold Street, Chesterfield Tel: 01246 273091. Meal offers. Wheelchair access.

The Jolly Farmer, Heath Road, Holmewood, Chesterfield Tel: 01246 855608. Meal offers Monday – Friday lunchtimes.

The New Inn, Mansfield Road, Chesterfield Tel: 01246 273727. Meal offers Monday – Saturday lunchtimes. Wheelchair access.

On the A619 between Chesterfield and Baslow is: **The Highwayman, Baslow Road, Eastmoor, Chesterfield S42 7DA** Tel: 01246 566330. A large roadside hostelry offers pensioners a two course lunch (starter and main course) Monday – Saturday at £5.99. Coaches welcome. Disabled access.

The Somerset House, 1 Top Road, Calow, Chesterfield S44 5AF Tel: 01246 278225. A traditional family-run pub two miles from Chesterfield town centre and next to the Royal Hospital, Calow. Sheila Linton ensures a good welcome for her customers. Home made steak pie, lasagne, cod & chips at £3.95 lunchtime – teatime, Monday – Saturday. Vegetarians catered for. Tea and coffee served. Disabled access and toilets. Coaches and mini-buses welcome by appointment.

The Spital, Spital Lane, Chesterfield Tel: 01246 204998. Meal offers Monday – Friday. Wheelchair access from the side tap-room bar.

The Welbeck Inn, Soresby Street, Chesterfield Tel: 01246 271643. Meal offers Monday – Saturday.

The White Horse, High Street, Old Whittington, Chesterfield Tel: 01246 450414. Offer on two course meals Monday – Friday 12 noon – 5pm. Wheelchair access.

CHINLEY

Chinley is half-way between Buxton and Glossop on the A6. It is a large village with stone-built Victorian buildings on the western edge of the National Park. The Old Hall Inn was built in the 16th century as the home of the Kyrke family. Charles Wesley was a frequent visitor. The industrial revolution brought three mills along the Blackbrook and the Peak Forest tramway, where horse-drawn wagons were used to carry stone from Dove Holes to the nearby canal at Buxworth. Map B2.

The Lamb Inn, Hayfield Road, Chinley, High Peak SK23 6AL Tel: 01663 750519. If your idea of a perfect place to lunch is in an olde-worlde pub, built in 1762, with open fires and a friendly atmosphere you will love The Lamb Inn. Allan and Dorothy Atkinson serve excellent food, including vegetarian options which are offered every day. It is home-cooked and fresh vegetables are served with all meals. Tea and coffee served. The over-60's meal deal is available Mondays – Fridays 12 noon – 2.30pm and a typical example of a three course meal would be home made soup, Roast leg of lamb finishing with rhubarb crumble, sherry trifle etc. A three course meal costs £6.75, two courses are £5.50. There is wheelchair access but toilets are up a short flight of stairs. Coaches and mini buses are catered for by arrangement. Situated on the A62 between Chinley and Hayfield.

CLAY CROSS

This mainly industrial town is on the A61 and is 6 miles south of Chesterfield. George Stephenson, when driving a tunnel under Clay Cross hill, discovered a rich seam of coal. 400 houses were built for the navvies working on the railway. By 1857 the small village population had grown to 2,278 people. The mines have long since closed but the local shops thrive and a market is held on Saturdays. Map F5.

The Cannon, Thanet Street, Clay Cross Tel: 01246 250078. Meal offers Monday – Friday. Wheelchair access from rear of building.

The Clay Oven Tandoori Restaurant, High Street, Clay Cross Tel: 01246 863307. 10% discount and 20% discount for take away orders.

Now a World Heritage Site, it is where Sir Richard Arkwright built the first cotton mill in Derbyshire in 1771 in partnership with Jedediah Strutt. Masson Mill has a working mill museum

in addition to a retail shopping park. North Street, built in 1776, has two rows of millworker's cottages consisting of three rooms, one above the other. Living and cooking space on the ground floor, sleeping on the first floor, with a workroom for the husband on the top floor with light for his hand-weaving – the women and children worked in the mills. On the Promenade is Scarthin Books – an excellent secondhand bookshop which offers tea, coffee and light snacks. Map E6.

Cromford Garden Centre, Derby Road, Cromford Lunches for pensioners Monday – Friday at £4.50. Vegetarian alternatives available. Tea and coffee served. Coaches and mini-buses welcome at any time without appointments.

Greyhound Hotel, Market Place, Cromford Tel: 01629 822551. Built by Sir Richard Arkwright in 1776 to house visitors to the mill. Meal offer Monday – Friday lunchtime. Tea and coffee. Disabled access.

DARLEY DALE

Between the market town of Bakewell and Matlock town lies Darley Dale, surrounding by countryside and just a few minutes drive from the Chatsworth Estate and the pretty villages of Stanton and Rowsley. It is home to the Peak Village Retail Outlet should you feel in need of some retail therapy. Darley Dale is made up of several smaller settlements, namely Churchtown, Darley Bridge or South Darley, Darley Hillside, Northwood and Two Dales. Two Dales is where the well known local writer Crichton Porteous lived. Darley Dale remains forever associated with the pioneering engineer Sir Joseph Whitworth, famous inventor of the true plane and the Whitworth thread for nuts and bolts. Born in Stockport in 1803, Joseph Whitworth served his apprenticeship in his uncle's cotton mill before setting up his engineering business in Manchester. He introduced the first standard gauges, taps, dies and planing machines and became an extremely wealthy industrialist. He bought Stancliffe Hall on the eastern slopes of the Dale where he spent the last fifteen years of his life. His widow also founded the Whitworth Hospital. The church was founded around 900 AD and almost entirely rebuilt after the Norman Conquest. Parts of the 12th century fabric remain, along with some earlier Celtic and Saxon stonework, excellent Norman masonry, and a selection of ancient stone coffins in and around the porch. Directly opposite the main porch entrance stands the famous Darley Yew, a tree reputed to be two thousand years old with an enormous girth of 33 feet. The Red House Carriage Museum houses a unique collection of horse-drawn conveyances. Adjacent to Whitworth Park is Darley Dale Station where steam train buffs can buy a ticket and climb aboard at weekends throughout the year courtesy of Peak Rail, a group of dedicated enthusiasts who have earned Heritage Railway status. A four mile section of the former Midland Railway line has been reconstructed between the old rail-head at Rowsley and Matlock Station. Map E6.

Darley Dale Fish Bar, Broadwalk, Darley Dale Meal offer.

Fir Trees Garden Centre, Darley Dale, Matlock If you are a keen gardener you couldn't do better than combining a morning's shopping for plants rounded off by lunch at the coffee shop. Beautifully cooked, home-made food and a wide selection of non-alcoholic drinks in a very comfortable and relaxed setting. The gift shop has plenty of variety and is perfect for finding those out-of-the-ordinary presents taking the stress out of buying Christmas and birthday gifts. Lunches from £3 for senior citizen's on production of your Gold Card.

The Grouse Inn, Dale Road North, Darley Dale, Matlock DE4 2FT Tel: 01629 734357. Meal offers. Tea and coffee.

Pickford's House Museum, Derby

The cathedral city still retains its Viking name – Deorbus. The cathedral has a fine early 16th century tower but the remainder of the building was rebuilt to the designs of James Gibbs. It contains the tomb of Bess of Hardwick – founder of the Cavendish dynasty and the Earls and Dukes of Devonshire. The city boasts a fine museum and art gallery with a collection of paintings by Joseph Wright and the Royal Crown Derby china works has a visitors centre. The Industrial Museum and Pickfords House, a museum of 18th century life are also worth a visit. Map F8.

Acropolis Coffee Bar, Market Place, Derby. Meal offer Monday – Friday lunchtimes.

George's Tradition Fish & Chips, Park Farm Centre,

Allestree 10% discount per meal.

George's Tradition Fish & Chips, Hollybrook Way, Heatherton Village 10% discount per meal.

Grangecraft Garden Centre Restaurant, Hospital Lane, Mickleover Meal offer Thursday.

Swiss Cottage Restaurant, Audley Centre, Derby Meal offer.

The Clock Tower Restaurant at Derby Garden Centre, Alfreton Road, Little Eaton Tel: 01332 831666. Meal offer Tuesday 12 noon – 2.30pm. Tea and coffee. Wheelchair access and disabled toilet.

The Flowerpot, 23-25 King Street, Derby DE1 3DZ Tel: 01332 204955, Offer smaller portions at lower prices to pensioners on all meals.

The Greyhound, Village Street, Derby Tel: 01332 273637. A community public house offering a selection of home-made food. All main meals are two for £7.00 Monday – Friday 12 noon – 7pm, Saturday & Sunday 12 noon – 3pm, Sunday carvery. Tea and coffee. Disabled access. Coaches and mini-buses by arrangement.

The Jonty Farmer, Kedleston Road, Derby Tel: 01332 292312. Simon and Sue always give a warm welcome and several senior citizens have commented on the superb food. 20% off main menu prices Monday – Thursday.

The Old Marina Bar & Restaurant, Shardlow Marina, Derby Tel: 01332 799797. Meal offer Monday – Friday 12 noon – 2.30pm & 6pm – 7.30pm and Saturday 12 noon – 2.30pm.

Opposite the parish church on Church Street is a long, low, five-bayed cruck building now converted to shops. The Green Dargon Inn has medieval origins, and was until 1547, a chantry for the Guild of the Blessed Virgin Mary. The High Street has a barn with a carved king post roof and may have been a 15th century house. The area was prosperous in the 16th-18th centuries, witnessed by the surviving number of fine buildings from these periods. Coal mining was started at Stubley in in 1640 and a dyeing factory was situated in Soaper Lane. Other local industires included tanning, soap, scythes and other edged tools. Map F4.

The Bridge Inn, Sheffield Road, Dronfield Special offer on beers. They do not serve food.

The Old Potting Shed Coffee Shop, Ward's Garden Centre, Coal Aston Meal offer Tuesday.

DUFFIELD

Henry de Ferrers built a huge castle here in the 11th century, but his descendant, Robert, became involved in two schemes to overthrow Henry II. The building was demolished and the site is now called Castle Hill. Charles I sold the manor, which came into the possession of Thomas Newton who built the present Hall in the 1620's. It is now the headquarters of the Derbyshire Building Society. Map F8.

Lord Scarsdale, New Zealand Lane, Duffield, Belper Tel: 01332 841156. Meal offers Monday – Saturday 12 noon – 2pm. On Monday afternoons they show classic films. For that special occasion they will prepare a specific dish with 48 hours notice. Wheelchair access via one small step.

ETWALL

Nestling among little hills the 17th century hall was built from the ruins of Tutbury Castle and has gates by Robert Bakewell. The church is by a charming group of almshouses adorned with heraldic panels and two sundials on the chimney stacks. The wells are dressed in May. Map E9.

The Hawk and Buckle, 40 Main Street, Etwall, Derby DE65 6LP Tel: 01283 733471. Formerly known as the Cotton Arms, its present name comes from the buckled hawk on the family's coat of arms. It dates from the early 19th century. Clive and Cheryl MaIntyre took over the pub in 1998 and always make you feel welcome. No special deals for senior citizens but meals start at £3.95 at all times. Wheelchair access through archway to rear of building.

EYAM

Known famously as the 'Plague Village' – and thousands of visitors flock here from all over the world, fascinated by the valiant story of sacrifice which the village has to tell. The legacy left by the plague is still evidenced throughout this close-knit community where many of the descendents of the plague survivors still reside. Commemorative plaques to the victims are displayed on the walls of the cottages where they lived – and died – and their heroic tale is related to visitors in vivid pictorial displays at both the Parish Church and at the Eyam Museum on Hawkhill Road at the western end of the village. Map D3.

The Miners Arms, Eyam Tel: 01433 630853. Situated in a quiet backwater, this hostelry was built in 1630. Until 1764 it was known as the Kings Head when it was renamed as the lead miners held their Barmote courts here. Ian Jackson and Jessica Wales provide delicious freshly prepared lunches Monday-Friday. Wheelchair access. It is reputedly the most haunted building in Derbyshire, though most customers say the only spirits they see come in glasses!

Fairfield

Near Buxton, but it keeps its individual character with one of the highest golf courses in the country at 1200 feet. Just beyond the common is Water Swallows Green where a stream disappers into the earth and rises again three miles away in Chee Dale. Map B4.

The Devonshire Arms, North Road, Fairfield, Buxton Tel: 01298 22148. Meal offers. Wheelchair access. Overlooking the golf course. Map B4.

FLAGG

Off the beaten track and in the middle of beautiful countryside Flagg is known for Flagg Races which take place at Easter every year. Map C6.

Edge Close Farm Tearooms, Edge Close Farm, Flagg SK17 9QT Tel: 01298 85144 Situated in converted farm buildings, it is open Thursday – Sunday. If you want a really good, all day breakfast, farmhouse style, this is the place to go but they don't stop there. All food is freshly cooked on the premises and they offer a variety of food, from sandwiches to steaks. Home made cakes and cream teas make it the perfect place for that mid-afternoon stop. Delicious home-made jams and chutneys are also on sale. Lunches served Saturday– Sunday – steak pie, beef hotpot, stew and dumplings, etc. Vegetarian alternatives. Fully licensed to serve alcohol. There are toilets for people with disabilities and the car parking area is level. Coach parties are welcome but you would need to book.

Duke of York Inn, Ashbourne Road, Flagg, Buxton Tel: 01298 72727. Situated on a turnpike road, it was opened in 1618.

Meal offers.

The Plough Inn, Flagg Tel: 01298 85557. Meal offers on Thursdays.

FOOLOW

The village green is complete with duck pond, stone cross, bull-ring, and an ancient well enclosed on three sides by a stone wall. This upland village lying at 1,000 feet above sea-level can hardly ever have been more attractive throughout the seven hundred years of it's history, than it is today. Of the original five inns survives the Bull's Head. Map D3.

The Bull's Head Inn, Foolow, Hope Valley Tel: 01433 630873 offers traditional English food in a friendly, family run pub. Pensioners' special offer lunches are served Tuesday – Friday lunchtimes. Tea and coffee available. Vegetarian food is also offered. Coaches and mini-buses are welcome with small numbers. Flat access from the car park and disabled toilets.

GLOSSOP

A small town approached by a long stretch of road beside Kinder Scout and once famous for printing calico and making paper. One of the first mills here, Rolfes Mill in Wesley Street, was built in 1785. The railway arrived in the 1840's and Glossop was created a borough in 1866. The Heritage Centre is on the square opposite the Market Hall. Some of the older haunts remain – gabled houses climb the road beside the church and the tall market cross in the square. Map B2.

The George Hotel, Norfolk Street, Glossop SK13 7QU Tel: 01457 855449. Centrally situated in the heart of Glossop, this hotel is personally supervised by Juliette Palmer providing excellent home-cooked food and a high level of service. Lunches available 12 noon – 2pm Monday – Thurs6day. Two courses costs £4.95 and three £5.95. Vegetarian options are available. Tea and coffee served. Disabled access and toilets. Coaches by appointment.

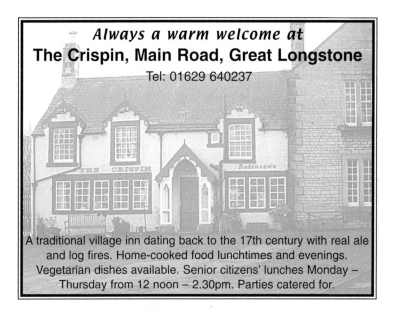

GREAT LONGSTONE

Approached from the west along a fine avenue of elm trees, the
road twists gently downwards into the village past the Manor
House and the 18th century Crispin Inn, to what must once
have been a large village green. Markets were held here from
the Middle Ages, and until a century ago an annual fair took
place on the green each September during Wakes Week. A
medieval market cross stands in the centre of the Green
opposite and just below the gated entrance to Longstone Hall.
Originally stone built around 1600 the Hall was rebuilt in brick
in 1747 by Thomas Wright, whose family have lived in the
village for 700 years, and occupied the Hall for 400 years until
1929. Map D4.

The Crispin, Main Road, Great Longstone Tel: 01629 640237.
A traditional village inn dating back to the 17th century serving
home-cooked food lunchtimes and evenings. Real ale and log
fires. Vegetarian dishes available. Tea and coffee served. Two

61

course senior citizens' lunches at £5.95 from Monday – Thursday from 12 noon – 2.30pm. Parties catered for. Coaches and mini-buses by arrangement.

GRINDLEFORD

The village includes Padley on the west bank of the river Derwent. Padley Hall, now ruined, was once the residence of the Eyre family. Padley Chapel on the upper floor of the gate-house was restored in 1933 to commemorate two Catholic priests, Nicholas Garlick and Robert Ludlam, who were arrested here in 1588. Theye were taken to Derby where they were hung, drawn and quartered. A pilgrimage takes place every July to the chapel in memory of the martyrs. Facing the chapel is Brunt's Barn, opened in 1981 as a wild flower nursery. An ideal walking centre for Burbage and Froggatt edges. The café by the station sells Grindleford Spring Water. Map D4.

Sir William Hotel, Grindleford Tel: 01433 630303. Enlarged after the railway came when it was named the Commercial Hotel, it changed its name in the early 20th century. Famous dishes include Norfolk Country Pie and the Fisherman's Crumble. Meal offer Monday – Friday lunchtimes. Wheelchair access.

North Lees Hall, Hathersage

Charlotte Bronte visited here in 1845 and features it as 'Norton' in *Jane Eyre* and North Lees Hall is where the Rivers sisters lived. (See *An Accessible Wilderness: Life at Stanage and the North Lees Estate* by Jen Edgar. Derbyshire County Council 2003) The Eyre family were once large landowners in the district. Legend says that Little John, friend of Robin Hood, is buried in the churchyard. Until the 18th century, the village was known for

making brass buttons and wire, but in 1750 Henry Cocker founded that Atlas works for wire making. Needle and pin makers followed and a paper mill was opened at North Lees. Wire and needle making moved to Sheffield and the last mill closed in 1902. Map D3.

The Plough Inn, Leadmill Bridge, Hathersage, Hope Valley S32 1BA Tel: 01433 650319. Bob and Cynthia Emery welcome you to their inn with 16th century origins set in 9 acres by the River Derwent. Real fires and beamed ceilings add to the charm. The offer smaller portions of meals at lower prices Monday – Friday lunchtimes – many people comment 'not just pub-grub'. Wheelchair access.

HAYFIELD

This village is on the threshold of Kinder Scout on the banks of the River Sett and was once known for calico printing and paper-making. Birthplace of Arthur Lowe – Captain Mainwairing from BBC TV's *Dad's Army*. Map B3.

The Pack Horse, Market Street, Hayfield, High Peak SK22 2EP
Tel: 01663 740074. Dating from 1577, they serve lunches Monday – Friday. Disabled access.

A scattered village lying between the towns of Ripley, Ambergate and Belper, it comprises of two halves – Heage and Nether Heage. In former times, coalmines and ironworks existed at Morley Park and Butterley and were major employers. Morley Park has the stubby remains of two coke-fired blast furnaces – one built in 1780, the other in 1818. A POW camp was built at Nether Heage during the Second World War. Heage Hall was begun in the 15th century and is said to be haunted. Heage windmill has six sails and is a well-known landmark. It has recently been restored. The post box in the wall of the post office is rare – bearing the cypher of Edward VIII. It was at Belper that Jedediah Strutt built his cotton mills. Map F6.

The Black Boy, Old Road, Heage, Belper DE56 2BN Tel: 01773 856799, Built in the 1840's, this public house and first floor restaurant offers traditional home-cooked lunches for pensioners Monday – Saturday 12 noon – 2pm. On Sundays, smaller portions are available but it is essential to book. Vegetarian dishes are offered and tea and coffee is also served. Evening meals are served 6 – 8pm on Monday – Thursday and 6 – 9pm on Friday and Saturday. There are no facilities for disabled people. Coaches and mini-buses should pre-book.

A little hilltop market town once producing hosiery, coal, iron and pottery. Market days are Friday and Saturday. Samuel Watson, who died in 1715, is buried in the church. He is famous for much of the carving in Chatsworth House. Heanor is now combined with the smaller communities of Langley Mill, Marlpool, Codnor, Loscoe and Aldercar, around the sides of Heanor Hill. Map G8.

Crest of the Wave Fish & Chip Restaurant, Market Place, Heanor Meal offer.

Memory Lane Inn & Restaurant, Derby Road, Heanor Tel: 01773 534977. Meal offer lunchtimes.

The Mundy Arms, Ilkeston Road, Heanor DE75 7LX Tel: 01773 712715. A Hardys and Hansons pub run by the friendly Stephen Richards. Golden Years menu Monday – Friday lunchtimes. Vegetarian food served. Tea and coffee. Wheelchair access and disabled toilets. Coaches by arrangement.

HOLBROOK

A hilltop site with lovely views. Map F8.

Housed in a fine 18th century building is **The Wheel Inn, 14 Chapel Street, Holbrook, Belper DE56 0TQ** Tel: 01332 880006. Home cooked lunches 12 noon – 2pm Monday – Friday. £4.95 includes a free soup or coffee. The Hungarian chef provides cottage pie, chicken in a creamy stilton sauce, etc. Vegetarian choices are offered and tea and coffee are available. The Tradewinds menu offers dishes from around the world with Hungarian specials. There is disabled access. Coach parties and mini-buses by arrangement. Highly recommended.

HOPE

Dominated by Lose Hill and Win Hill on one side and cement works on the other. A mile north of the village at Brough is the site of a Roman fort, known by them as Anavio, on the Roman road to Glossop and Melandra Castle. In the village churchyard stands a 7 foot Saxon cross shaft. Map D2.

The Poachers Arms, 95 Castleton Road, Hope S33 6SB Tel: 01433 620380. Philip and Linda Wood offer meals at lunchtimes. Wheelchair access via ramp on patio into conservatory.

The Woodroffe Arms, Castleton Road, Hope S33 6SB Tel: 01433 620351. Parts of the building date back 400 years and it was formerly a coaching inn. Richard and Hannah serve freshly prepared home-made food from Tuesday – Thursday 12noon – 2.30pm. Real fires. Wheelchair access. Walkers and dogs always 6--9--welcome – not just during the quiet season!

The Bookstore, Ashbourne Road, Brierlow Bar SK17 9PY (Tel: 01298 71017) is on the A515 road to Buxton and is one of the largest in the country – and at 1,075ft – one of the highest. David McPhie always carries a large stock of books – 100,000 – in addition to CDs, gifts, O.S. maps and stationery. There is an indoor play area for the grandchildren and picnic tables outside. A boules court is for the use of customers and in the small woodland with its nestbox village, over 50 species of birds have been seen. Tel: 01298 71017.

The Bull i' th' Thorn, Hurdlow, Buxton Tel: 01298 83348. A Robinson's pub seating 120 people. Original flagstone floor, oak beams and lots of militaria and old furniture. A separate medieval room is available for private functions. All food is home-cooked and sourced locally with a vegetarian choice of 20 dishes. Meal offers Monday – Friday lunchtimes. Wheelchair access. Map B4.

The Market Place, Ilkeston

There are fine wide views from the hillside above the Erewash valley and the church-crowned hilltop is a landmark. Until recent years the major employment was in coalmines and the ironworks at Stanton and Staveley. These industries have been replaced by the textile industry, upholstery and lingerie. There is a stalls market on Thursday and Saturday. The area played an important part in the writings of DH Lawrence. The actor, Robert Lindsay, was born here and starred in *Me and My Girl* and *Horatio Hornblower*. Map G8.

Bath Street Fish Bar, Bath Street, Ilkeston Meal offer.

The Carpenters Arms, Dale Abbey, Ilkeston DE7 4PP Tel: 0115 932 5277 Built in 1880, the menu is short but it's great food! Monday – Friday lunchtimes offers haddock and chips at £3.95. Disabled access.

Handy for shoppers seeking a bargain at Armstrong's Mill is **The Dewdrop Inn, 24 Station Street, Ilkeston DE7 5TE** Tel: 0115 932 9684. Voted CAMRA pub of the year, this hostelry unchanged since 1880, offers cheese on toast, cheese cobs, bacon and home-made black pudding sandwich with brown sauce for around £1. 'The sandwiches are huge!' No meals – but this is like pubs used to be! Worth a special trip.

The White Cow, Nottingham Road, Ilkeston DE7 5NX Tel: 0115 930 4825. John and Carol Windmill always make you welcome in this Hardys and Hansons house dating from the early 19th century. No special deals for pensioners, but two meals for £8 must be a bargain! Disabled parking and toilets, wheelchair access. Brail and large print menu available – unique in Derbyshire? Many pensioners have commented on the welcoming and friendly atmosphere.

KEGWORTH

A small village on the border with Leicestershire.

The Cap and Stocking, 20 Borough Street, Kegworth DE74 2FF Tel: 01509 674814. One mile from junction 24 on the M1. This pub built in 1910 takes it's title from the former street name. Lunches are served Monday – Friday. No chips! Famous for their home-made sausages. Wheelchair access up two small steps.

Long Eaton

Eight miles east of Derby, the town lies close to the river Trent and straddles the border with Nottinghamshire. By the 19th century the village had grown with quarrying, small machine-made lace making and the coming of the railway in the 1850's. By the early 1900's the population with Sawley had exceeded 20,000 people. Joseph Pickford of Derby built the hall as a private residence and it serves as the Town Hall. One of the country's leading public schools, Trent College, was founded in 1868. Trent Lock, an easy stroll from the town, is a centre for sailing and boating. Map G9.

George's Tradition Fish & Chips, Wilsthorpe Road, Long Eaton 10% discount.

Shots Wine Bar, Gibb Street, Long Eaton Tel: 0115 946 1131. Meal offer Monday – Saturday 10am – 3pm.

LONGNOR

Although technically in Staffordshire, the village of Longnor is a delightful place to visit and couldn't be left out of the guide! Surrounded by beautiful scenery, the village itself has tiny cottages, narrow lanes and a friendly atmosphere. A favourite with hikers and walkers, it has a craft centre in the old Market Hall and you can walk off your lunch wandering the narrow side streets that will take you back to a less hurried pace of life. A visit in September will give you the chance to see the spectacular well-dressings. Map B4.

Ye Old Cheshire Cheese, Longnor, Buxton SK17 ONS Tel: 01298 83218. If it's character you're after then this pub has it by the yard. Excellent food, particularly their roast dinners, are served in the bar or in the dining room. Special offers for senior citizens are offered on Tuesdays and Fridays with a two course meal for two people for £7.

Stretching for two miles are Matlock Bath, Matlock Dale, Matlock Bridge, Matlock Town and Matlock Bank. The Romans mined lead here but the town grew to prominence in 1698 when the first bath was built over a warm spring. There is a mining museum at Matlock Bath and a cable-car ride to the Heights of Abraham. The area once had over forty hydropathic establishments, treating the sick and infirm. John Smedley built his great hydro on Matlock Bank and it now serves as the County Hall. His former home, Riber Castle, is now a ruin on the skyline over 850 feet above sea-level. Map E6.

JET's Coffee Shop & Restaurant, Matlock Garden Centre Tel: 01629 580500. Meal offer from Gardener's Choice menu Monday – Friday from 12 noon – 2.30pm. Tea and coffee. Disabled Access. Coaches and mini-buses by arrangement.

Matlock Green Fish Bar, Matlock Meal offer.

Riber Hall Hotel, Matlock Tel: 01629 582795. 10% discount weekday lunchtimes.

Scotland Nurseries Garden Centre, Tansley 10% discount on food Tuesday at The Heathers Café & Restaurant.

The Coach House, Main Road, Lea Tel: 01629 534346. Set in old farmbuildings and renowned for their home made Jersey ice cream. Three course lunch £6.95 Wednesday – Saturday lunchtimes. Wheelchair access via small steps.

The Crown, Crown Square, Matlock. Tel: 01629 580991. Part of the Wetherspoon Group. Varied menu including low fat and vegetarian. Senior citizens 10am – 10pm daily. They serve tea and coffee. Facilities for people with disabilities. Coaches and mini-buses by appointment.

The Horseshoes, 81 Matlock Green, Matlock DE4 3BX Tel: 01629 592911. A stone-built former coaching inn run by James and Mandy Hilton has been a public house since 1821. It boasts the oldest public toilet in Derbyshire – disused, and is reputedly haunted by several friendly ghosts. They offer an extensive vegetarian and fish menu and tea and coffee are served. Lunches Monday – Saturday 12 noon – 2.30pm and on Sunday

12 noon – 1pm. One course is £4, two £5, and three at £6.00. Starters range from homemade soup to garlic mushrooms and Yorkshire pudding and gravy. Main courses include roast of the day, cod and chips, homemade pie, sausage and mash with onion gravy, cottage pie and vegetable lasagne. Disabled access is gained from the rear of the building and groups of ten or more people are welcome by arrangement.

MAYFIELD

A small village on the borders of Derbyshire and Staffordshire. It consists of three parts – Upper Mayfield, with some lovely 17th and 18th century houses, Lower Mayfield with church and yarn mill by the river Dove, and the main part of the village in the middle. The poet, Thomas Moore lived at Moore Cottage, formerly Stancliffe Farm. His daughter, Olivia Byron Moore, died on 18 March 1815 and was buried in the churchyard. Lord Byron was a guest at Mayfield several times. Ideal stopping place for Alton Towers. Map D8.

The Royal Oak Hotel, Mayfield Road, Upper Mayfield, Ashbourne DE6 2BN Tel: 01335 300090. This family-run establishment lies at the west end of the town and dates from the 17th century. Food is sourced locally and freshly cooked to order by the owner, Jan Snelling, assisted by her daughter-in-law Christelle. Lunches Monday – Friday 12 noon – 2.30pm. Wheelchair access. Parking. Ideal as a stop-off for Dovedale and Alton Towers.

The Rose and Crown, Main Road, Middle Mayfield, Ashbourne DE6 2JT Tel: 01335 342498. No specific menu for pensioners but dishes can be had for £5.95. No dogs – guide dogs only.

MICKLEOVER

Just SW of Derby but still retaining a village feel, in spite of being absorbed by the city in 1968, it still has some attractive old buildings. Oliver Cromwell reputedly stayed at The Old Hall in Orchard Street. The Great Northern Railway arrived in 1876 and Mickleover hasn't stopped growing since – the station is now a mile from the centre of the village! Map F8.

The Masons Arms, 1 Etwall Road, Mickleover, Derby DE3 0DL Tel: 01332 513156. Trevor and Nadine Price welcome you to their olde-worlde pub. Lunches Monday – Friday 12 noon – 2pm. Tea and coffee.

The Vine Inn, 20 Uttoxeter Road, Mickleover, Derby DE3 5DA Tel: 01332 513956. A Victorian pub dating from 1846. Lunches for pensioners from £1.50 – £3.95 Monday – Friday 12 noon – 2pm. Vegetarian dishes, tea and coffee served. Wheelchair access. Coaches and mini-buses by arrangement.

NEW MILLS

New Mills is 6 miles from Chapel-en-le-Frith and 8 miles from Stockport.It lies on the borders of NW Derbyshire and Cheshire and traces its history back to the 13th century when a corn mill was established. In the 18th century five cotton mills were built around the Torrs, a sandstone ridge running through the town on the banks of two rivers – the Sett and the Goyt. The mills ceased working in the early 1900's and the former derelict site is now The Torrs Riverside Park, for recreation and relaxation. The New Mills Heriatge Centre was opened to promote tourism. Map B3.

The Royal Oak, Market Street, New Mills. Tel: 01663 743675. Reasonably priced home-cooked food. Wheelchair access via one small step.

OCKBROOK

A quiet village 4 miles east of Derby. The Moravian settlement was founded in 1750 and was a great influence on John Wesley. This was one of three settlements in England founded by a Christian sect originating in Germany. The school was built in 1799 and is now a boarding establishment for girls. Ockbrook village was once a textile centre and some cottages still show the long lines of framework knitters windows in their upper storeys. There are fine views over the Trent and Derwent valleys into Nottinghamshire and Leicestershire. Map G8.

The Queen's Head, Victoria Avenue, Ockbrook DE72 3RN Tel: 01332 674151. Leighton and Joan Seabrook with their daughter Sally and husband, Adam, provide home-made produce and fresh fish for their numerous customers. They offer a pensioners menu Monday – Saturday 12 noon – 2.30pm. You will need to book at weekends. Choose from a starter and main course or main course and sweet for £5.50. Haddock, scampi, gammon steak, steak and kidney pie and Spanish lamb all feature on the menu. Tea and coffee. Wheelchair access and disabled toilet.

PILSLEY

Situated six miles from Chesterfield – not to be confused with the Pilsley near Chatsworth House. The coal mines have gone and there is a little modern church with a fine peace memorial showing a bronze trumpeting angel holding a wreath. Map G6.

The Herb Garden, Hall View Cottage, Hardstoft, Pilsley, Chesterfield S45 8AH Tel: 01246 854268. Just the place to find that elusive herb you have always wanted! The conservatory tearoom does not do special deals for senior citizens, but with food of this quality, and at these prices, you are hardly likely to quibble. Sandwiches, jacket potatoes, teacakes, scone and cakes. Tea and coffe. Disabled access.

RIPLEY

Once famous for the Butterley Ironworks where the roof for London's St Pancras Station was made. At nearby Pentrich in the hard years after Waterloo, starving weavers and stockingers turned rebels – three were hanged and the remainder transported. Denby Pottery Visitor Centre, Derby Road, Denby DE5 8NX is on the B6179, south of the town. Miuseum and guided factory tours from Monday – Thursday 10.30am to 1pm and the factory shop is open Monday – Saturday 9am – 5pm. The Midland Railway Centre is at Butterley Station. Map F7.

Crest of the Wave Fish & Chip Restaurant, New Street, Ripley Meal offer.

The Devonshire Arms, Pentrich Lane End, Buckland Hollow nr Ripley Tel: 01773742661. Meal offer. Wheelchair access difficult but the staff are willing to help.

The Moss Cottage Hotel, Nottingham Road, Ripley DE5 3JT Tel: 01773 742555. Lunch Monday – Friday. Choice of three starters, five main courses and three sweets. Two courses £3.95 or three courses for £5.95. Wheelchair access and disabled toilet.

ROWORTH

The Little Mill Inn, Roworth, Glossop Good value for money – two courses for £4.75 and three for £5.85. All home-made food and excellent service. Map B2.

SCROPTON

Situated in the Dove Valley in the south of the county. It has always been an agricultural settlement. The churchyard contains 16 memorial headstones supplied by the Imperial War Graves Commission to mark graves of airmen from overseas who died whilst serving with the RAF Training Squad based at neaby Church Broughton airfield. Riding for the disabled operate a centre in Watery Lane. Where the Foston Brook meets the river Dove is a fine half-timbered house with gables. Map G5.

The Foresters Arms, Main Street, Scropton DE65 5PP Tel: 01283 812525. Colin Wilson serves good home-cooked food in this newly refurbished hostelry. £5.50 for two courses, lunchtimes Monday – Saturday. Tea and coffee. Disabled access. Dogs welcome. Coaches by appointment. Map

SHELDON

A small former lead-mining village 3 miles west of Bakewell off the A6 with stunning views over the surrounding countryside. The remains of the Magpie Mine are close by and can be visited by appointment. The mine was worked for over 300 years until 1924. It was taken over by the Peak District Historical Scoiety as a field centre. It is the most complete and interesting remains of a lead mine in the Peak District. Map D5.

The Cock and Pullet, Sheldon. The village pub was built from scratch in 1995, next to a former public house called the Devonshire Arms which had been closed for twenty years. Good old-fashioned atmosphere.

South Wingfield

South Wingfield Manor

This village is situated about two miles from Alfreton. Ralph Lord Cromwell, Lord Treasurer of England, began building the manor in 1441, and it was completed by the Talbot family who were Earls of Shrewsbury. The 6th Earl was the custodian of Mary Queen of Scots, and was the husband of Bess of Hardwick. Mary was held captive here in 1569 and 1584 – along with her retinue of 250 people! The house was dismantled during the civil war between Charles I and Cromwell and is now administered by English Heritage. Featured in the film *Jane Eyre* and on TV in *Peak Practice.* Tel: 01773 832060. Map F7.

The Old Yew Tree Inn, 51 Manor Road, South Wingfield, Alfreton DE55 7NH Tel: 01773 833763. An old country inn with real fires. Tea and coffee. Tuesday – Friday lunchtimes. Soup and a main course at £4.95. Wheelchair access by back door. Reputedly haunted by three ghosts.

STENSON

Located SW of Derby. From the A511 at the Cavendish look for Stenson Road. This takes you through Sunnyhill, Stenson fields and over the new A50 bridge to Stenson. The Trent and Mersey Canal was built through the parish of Twyford in 1796. The lock cottage was built in 1810. Stenson House, the largest building here, was built by Samuel Brown of Derby for Harpur-Crewe tenant Richard Forman. Map F9.

The Bubble Inn, Stenson Wharf, Stenson Road, Stenson, Derby DE73 1HL Tel: 01283 703113. The unusual name for this pub is taken from a local phenomenon – as the water re-enters the canal below the lock it tends to bubble from the outlet under the towpath. It is a popular canal-side pub in a 200 year-old converted barn. Lunches Monday – Saturday. Wheelchair access. Map E8.

STONEY MIDDLETON

A small village with cottages rising tier on tier on ledges of rock under hanging cliffs. The church is mainly 18th century but the tower was built in 1415 by Joan Eyre to commemorate her husband's safe return from Agincourt. In 1762 the jilted Hannah Baddaley flung herself from the cliffs but was saved by her voluminous skirts – it is now known as 'Lover's Leap'. There are several important pot-holes in the area, notably Carlswark Cavern. Map D4.

The Moon, Stoney Middleton Tel: 01433 630203. Situated on the A623, this old coaching house offers a large menu catering for all requirements. Starters, fish, grills, main courses, sweets. Specials board. It is advisable to book at weekends. Offers lunches for senior citizens Monday – Saturday 12 noon – 2.15pm. Vegetarian food available. Tea and coffee served. Disabled access. Coaches and mini-buses by appointment.

SWADLINCOTE

This large town in the south west of the county grew out of the coal and clay industries and is near the Staffordshire border, being about 3 miles from Burton upon Trent. Mentioned in the Domesday Book it was part of Church Gresley until 1846. In 1801 the population was 216 people which had risen to over 4,000 within a hundred years. The short-lived tram system operated between the years 1906 and 1927 when grand new shops were built in the High Street. Well worth a visit is the Sharps Pottery Heritage Museum which also houses the Magic Attic – a collection of thousands of old photographs and maps. Map

Falcon Restaurant, Rosliston Forestry Centre Meal offer Monday – Friday.

The Chesterfield at Hartshorne, Repton Road, Swadlincote Tel: 01283 217267. Meal offer 3pm – 6pm Monday – Saturday. Wheelchair access.

Swanwick

An old village whose population doubled in size to 5,000 during the 20th century. Silk hosiery was once produced here by framework knitters, but it was the Butterley Ironworks arrival in the 18th century which changed the face of Swanwick. Other industries were coal mining and boot and shoe making. Elizabeth Turner had a school built in 1740 for the education of 20 poor children. Swanwick hall was purchased by the county council in 1922 and opened as a school. Map F6.

The Steampacket, Derby Road, Swanwick, Alfreton DE55 1AB Tel: 01773 602172. Lunches on Thursdays only 12 noon – 2pm.

TADDINGTON

It is in the Derbyshire Dales close to Bakewell. This small village is popular with walkers and is one of the highest in the country. Close by is Five Wells, an ancient burial mound containing two tombs from the Neolithic period. At 1,400 feet, it is the highest megalithic tomb in England. Map C5.

Queens Arms, Main Road, Taddington, nr Buxton Tel: 01298 85245. Meal offers.

Snuggling into the west-facing hillside below High Ordish Ridge. Mills appeared in Lumsdale in what had been mainly an agricultural area and in the 19th century William Mycock had a hydro at what is now Tansley House. Later the village became known for nurseries and timber yards. Map E6.

The Gate Inn, The Knoll, Tansley, Matlock DE4 5FN Tel: 01629 583838. Offers lunches Monday – Saturday. Map E5.

The Gate Inn, Tansley in 1924

The mines have gone and have been replaced by services on the M1 at junction 29. Nearby Newton Hall was bulit in 1690. Map G6.

King Edward VII Hotel, High Street, Tibshelf, Alfreton Tel: 01773 591019. Meal offer Monday – Saturday.

Royal Oak, High Street, Tibshelf, Alfreton Tel: 01773 872257. Meal offer Tuesday – Friday 12 noon – 3pm. Tea and coffee. Wheelchair access and disabled toilet.

TISSINGTON

Known far and wide for its dressing of five wells at Ascensiontide, this village is sheer delight. Approached by an avenue of lime trees off the A515 the little stone houses gather around a green with the 16th century Hall and the old church. Map D7.

Tissington Hall

The Bluebell Inn, Tissington, Ashbourne, DE6 1NM Tel: 01335 350317. If country houses are your thing then Tissington Hall (open August – other times by arrangement Tel: 01335 350317) is a must and when you've finished wandering through the village why not stop off at The Bluebell Inn where you can buy traditional, home-cooked meals using local produce. There is something to suit everyone from grills to bar meals, banquets to

buffets and all dietary requirements are catered for i.e. gluten free, diabetic, dairy-free etc. Tea and coffee available. There is a large garden with easy access and car parking spaces and toilet facilities for people with disabilities. Offers for Senior Citizens are for parties of 15 or more and need to be booked in advance.

Tissington Church

WALTON ON TRENT

The village looks across the Trent to Staffordshire. Walton Hall, a lovely brick house of five bays, was built in 1720. Map D11.

The White Swan, Main Street, Walton on Trent, Swadlincote DE12 8LZ Tel: 01283 712378. No special deals for pensioners but two courses for £5.95 from 12 noon – 6pm Monday – Friday.

Florence Nightingale loved this village. Grey stone cottages built with materials from the local quarry. Come in May for the bluebells. Map E7.

Homesford Cottage Inn, Whatstandwell, Matlock Tel: 01629 822342. Meal offer Monday – Saturday lunchtimes. Two courses for £6.50 – starter and main course or main course and dessert. Good quality produce is always used – no frozen vegetables or 'cheap meat' here. There is a large choice of vegetarian food and tea and coffee are served. Disabled access is difficult as there is a step into the premises. Coaches and mini-buses by arrangement.

WILLINGTON

The village looks across meadows and the banks of the river Trent towards Repton. In the church porch at Repton is kept the old toll board for the five-arch bridge. This was one of the last main road bridges to be freed of tolls. Map E9.

The Green Dragon, The Green, Willington DE65 6BP Tel: 01283 702327. Situated 5 miles from Burton, this pretty 18th century pub is by the Trent and Mersey Canal and was formerly called The Navigation. The attractive interior is beamed with real fires. Jon Shaw serves plentiful food at reasonable prices. Wheelchair access.

Youlgrave

This quiet village, lying between the beautiful Bradford and Lathkill Dales, was once well known for its lead-mining. Those days have long gone and the village is now surrounded by farm land. The French artist, Lucien Pissaro, spent many painting holidays here. Be sure to visit the Norman church and, just a short drive away, the stone circles at Stanton and Harthill Moor. Map D6.

The Farmyard Inn, Main Street, Youlgrave, Bakewell, DE45 1UW Tel: 01629 636221. This olde worlde pub with an open fire is in the heart of the village. Between 5pm – 7pm, Monday – Friday, it offers a 'small portions' menu, ranging from rump steak to beef stew and a vegetarian option. There is disabled access and toilets. Coaches and mini-buses can be accommodated but please ring to arrange.

PLACES TO VISIT

Alton Towers Just over the border in Staffordshire – a great day out for the grandchildren.

Arbor Low Map D4. Derbyshire's Stonehenge – access at all times.

Arkwright's Cromford Mill, Cromford Map E6. Tel: 01629 624297. The world's first successful water-powered cotton spinning mill, now a World Heritage Site. Shops and restaurant. Open daily 9am – 5pm.

Bakewell Old House Museum Map D5. Open Easter to end of October 11am – 4pm. Tel: 01629 813642. A Tudor tax collector's house, rural life museum.

Belper, North Mill Map F6.

Blue John Cavern, Castleton S33 8WP Tel: 01433 620638. Map C2. Old mining equipment. The tour lasts 45 minutes.

Bolsover Castle Map G4. English Heritage.

Buxton Museum Map B3.

Calke Abbey, near Melbourne Tel: 01332 863822. National Trust. Map F9.

Calke Abbey

Castleton, Peveril Castle Map C2. English Heritage.

Caudwell's Mill, Rowsley Map E4. Open 1st March – 31st October, every day. November – February, weekends only. Tel: 01629 734374.

Chatsworth House and Garden Map E4. Home of the Duke of Devonshire. Open Easter to December 21st, 11am – 5.30pm. Tel: 01246 582204.

Chesterfield Museum Map F4.

Crich Tramway Village, near Matlock DE4 5DP Tel: 0870 75 87267. A re-created period street with unlimited tram rides for the entry fee. Map F6.

Denby Pottery Map F8.

Derby Cathedral & Visitor Centre Tel: 01332 341201. Map F4.

Derby Museum and Art Gallery Map F4. Tel: 01332 716659 with a collection of paintings by Joseph Wright.

Derby Royal Crown Derby Map F4. Tel: 01332 712800. China works has a museum and a visitors centre.

Derby The Industrial Museum Map F4. Tel: 01332 255308

Derby Pickfords House Museum, 41 Friargate Tel: 01332 255363. Map F4. A museum of 18th century life.

Devil's Arse – Peak Cavern, Castleton S33 8WS Tel: 01433 620285. Map C3. Set in a spectacular limestone gorge. Rope-making demonstration.

Kedleston Hall

Peak Rail, Matlock

Donington Grand Prix Collection, Donington Park, Castle Donington DE74 2RP Tel: 01332 811027. The largest collection of Grand Prix cars in the world.
Eyam Hall Map D3. Tel: 01433 631976. Built in 1671 and still lived in by the Wright family.

Hardwick Hall

Eyam Hall

Revolution House, Old Whittington, Chesterfield

Bolsover Castle

Glossop Heritage Centre, Henry Street, Glossop SK13 8BW
Tel: 01457 869176. Illustrates the history of the town. Map B1.
Gullivers Kingdom, Matlock Bath Map E5. Tel: 01629 580540.
Family theme park suitable for the grandchildren. Royal Cave.
Haddon Hall Map D4. Home of Lord Edward Manners. The
perfect medieval manor house – not to be missed! Open Easter
to end of September 10.30am – 4.30pm. Tel: 01629 814379.
Hardwick Hall Map G3. National Trust. Tel: 01246 850430.
Home of Bess of Hardwick.
Hardwick Old Hall Map G3. English Heritage. The ruined
home of Bess of Hardwick before she built the new hall.
Heights of Abraham, Matlock Bath Map E5. Tel: 01629 582365.
Cable car rides across the Derwent Valley. Tours in two show
caves.
Keddleston Hall Map E7. National Trust. Tel: 01332 842191.
Lea Gardens, Lea, near Matlock Map E5. Tel: 01629 534380. A
collection of rare rhododendrons, azaleas, alpines and conifers.
Garden shop and tea room. Home made cakes, tea and coffee.

Peveril Castle, Castleton

Matlock Bath Aquarium & Hollogram Gallery Map E5. Tel: 01629 583624. Site of original thermal baths with a collection of cold water, tropical and marine fish. Petrifying well. Gemstone collection.

Melbourne Hall Map F9.

Midland Railway Centre, Butterley Station, Ripley DE5 3QZ Tel: 01773 570140. A large collection of steam and diesel locomotives. Shop.

National Stone Centre, Wirksworth Map D6. Tel: 01629 824833. Story of stone exhibition. Gem panning. Shop. Open Easter – October 10.30am – 5pm and November – March 10am – 4pm.

New Mills Heritage Centre Map B1.

Peak District Mining Museum & Temple Mine, Matlock Bath Map E5. Tel: 01629 582834. History of lead mining in the Peak District.

Peak Rail, Matlock Station DE4 3NA Tel: 01629 580381. Map E5.

Sutton Scarsdale

Revolution House, Old Whittington, Chesterfield Tel: 01246 345727. Map F5.

South Wingfield Manor Map F6. English Heritage.

Speedwell Cavern, Winnats Pass, Castleton S33 8WA Tel: 01433 620512. Map C3. 105 steps down to meet your tour guide's boat for a glide through a 200 year-old lead mine.

Steeple Grange Light Railway, Wirksworth Map E7.

Sudbury Hall & the Musuem of Childhood Tel: 01283 585305. Map C8. National Trust.

Sutton Scarsdale, Chesterfield English Heritage

Swadlincote, Sharps Pottery Heritage Museum Map

Tissington Hall Tel: 01335 352200. Map D7. Home of Sir Richard FitzHerbert Bt.

Treak Cliff Cavern, Castleton S33 8WP Tel: 01433 620571. Map C3. Blue John is also mined here. Stalactites and stalagmites.

Sudbury Hall

Wirksworth Heritage Centre, Crown Yard, Wirksworth DE4 4ET Tel: 01629 825225. Housed in a former silk mill are displays of lead mining, well dressing and church clipping. Map E6.

TOURIST INFORMATION CENTRES

ASHBOURNE
13 Market Place
Ashbourne
Derbyshire DE6 1EU
Tel: 01335 343666
Fax: 01335 300638
e-mail: ashbourneinfo
@derbyshiredales.gov.uk

BAKEWELL
Old Market Hall
Bridge Street
Bakewell
Derbyshire DE45 IDS
Tel: 01629 813227
Fax: 01629 814782
e-mail: bakewell
@peakdistrict'npa.gov.uk

BURTON UPON TRENT
Coors Visitor Centre
Horninglow Street
Burton upon Trent
Staffordshire DE14 1YQ
Tel: 01283 508111 or 508112
Fax: 01283 517268
e-mail: tic@eaststaffsbc.gov.uk

BUXTON
The Crescent
Buxton
Derbyshire SK17 6BQ
Tel: 01298 25106
Fax: 0129873153
e-mail: tourism
@high peak.gov.uk

CHESTERFIELD
Rykneld Square
Chesterfield
Derbyshire S40 1SB
Tel: 01246 345777 or 345778
Fax: 01246 345770
e-mail: tourism
@chesterf ield.gov.uk

DERBY
Assembly Rooms
Market Place
Derby
Derbyshire DEI 3AH
Tel: 01332 255802
Fax: 01332 256137
e-mail: tourism@derby.gov.uk

GLOSSOP
The Gatehouse
Victoria Street
Glossop
Derbyshire SK13 8HT
Tel: 01457 855920
Fax: 01427 855920
e-mail: info
@glossoptouristcentre.co.uk

LEEK
1, Marketplace
Leek
Staffordshire ST13 5HH
Tel: 01538483741
Fax: 01538 483743
e-mail: tourism.services
@staffsmoorlands.gov.uk

MACCLESFIELD
Macclesfield Town Hall
Macclesfield
Cheshire SK10 1DX
Tel: 01625 504114 or 504115
Fax: 01625 504116
e-mail: Informationcentre

@macclesfield.gov.uk

MATLOCK
Crown Square
Matlock
Derbyshire DE4 3AT
Tel: 01629 583388
Fax: 01629 584131
e-mail: matlockinfo
@derbyshi redales.gov.uk

MATLOCK BATH
The Pavillion
Matlock
Derbyshire DE4 3NR
Tel: 01629 55082
Fax: 01629 56304
e-mail: matlockbathinfo
@derbyshiredales.gov.uk

RIPLEY
Town Hall
Market Place
Ripley
Derbyshire DE5 3BT
Tel: 01773 841488 or 841486
Fax: 01773 841487
e-mail: touristinformation
@ambervalley.gov.uk

SHEFFIELD
Visitor Information Point
Winter Garden
Sheffield
Tel: 01142211900
e-mail: visitor@sheffield.gov.uk

We plan to update this book on a regular basis, so if we have omitted your favourite place, then please let us know. We would also like to know if any details in this book have changed since going to press. We welcome your recommendations for establishments that offer special deals for Senior Citizens anywhere in the country – not just Derbyshire, as this is the first of a series of guides covering the country. You can contact us at:

Jen Edgar
Senior Citizens' Good Food Guide
184 Brown Edge Road, Buxton, Derbyshire SK17 7AA

Dick Richardson
Senior Citizens' Good Food Guide
Courtyard Cottage, Little Longstone, Bakewell, Derbyshire
DE45 1NN

GOLD CARD

The Gold Card is a discount scheme exclusively for Derbyshire residents who are aged 60 or over or who have certain types of disability. Gold Cards are free and are issued by district and borough council offices and some post offices. They also function as a bus pass. The Gold Card scheme is jointly funded and administered by Derbyshire County Council, Derby City Council and all the district councils of Derbyshire. For an application form please call 08 456 058 058.